HEALTHCARE HEROES

from illness to recovery

Dr Mark Rickenbach

Tim Saunders Publications

TS

Tim Saunders Publications

With thanks to those healthcare heroes working in the UK National Health System. With special mention to all those on the Southampton General Hospital vascular (D4), cardiothoracic (B2), and High Dependency wards. And also, to the Southampton hospital at home nurse team, the community primary care team, my family and especially my wife Louise.

CONTENTS

PREFACE

I do hope you enjoy some of the poems and prose that follows here. There is a chronological order to these which follows unexpected illness, admission to hospital and eventual surgery over the period November 2022 to February 2023.

I worked on hospital wards for eight years in the UK and abroad before thirty years as a GP, so this may flavour my patient perspective. Do dip in an out as you wish or whatever feels right to you.

Dr Mark Rickenbach

NURSES QUIET HEROISM – EVERY DAY

As nurses you are so cool, confident, and calm
coping with all the day's events
each an oasis of reassurance and help
amidst the rough terrain of illness, all around.

A ready smile in eyes above the mask,
a cheery comment to nudge the minutes by
they carry us along and get us through each day
as we await the twists and turns of fate.

Long twelve-hour shifts, run from eight to eight
breaks or meals threatened by the busy pace
an admission here, a fall nearby,
a tearful moment too
upset and anger, handled with a self-effacing calm.

So, we must value what we have
quiet heroism occurring every day
at work they take on all our problems
we, in turn, must support our nurses
in every way we can.

Dec 2022

*And the first conversation of the day with the
heroes on the ward is often about the weather
and trip in to work, as outlined next.*

DR MARK RICKENBACH

DRIVING INTO WORK

Thick frost upon the glass
wrinkled like older skin
the scraper cuts through
tracks across the frozen waste.

Plumes of white flakes scatter
and fall upon hands and sleeve
inside the same
but now upon the seats and coat.

Her misty face appears
through coated glass
approaching nearer, it seems
as melting moisture clears.

Calm and ready for work
she holds a slice of toast in hand
freshly buttered
another melting moment.

Crafted by hand that bread
freshly baked from tin
warm and slightly moist
a dream to savour, in the mouth.

Within this car, is a treasured jewel

sparkling with life and energy
serene in sampling her existence
broad smile lighting up the world.

Her shoes may clutter halls
and bag upon the stairs may trip
but we treasure every moment
and shared vibrancy of her being.

For she is our daughter
from giggling baby to happy toddler
adventurous teen to loving youth
and now she's driving out to hospital work.

January 2022

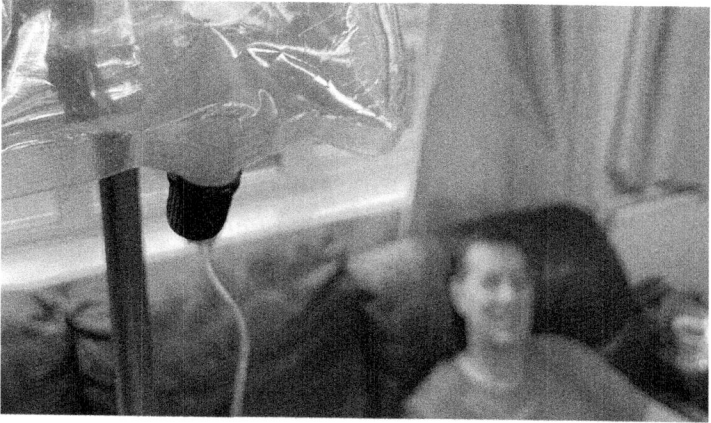

A DRIP IN THE OCEAN

Above me hangs a fluid bag
a tube runs down to meet my arm
lifesaving antibiotics float along, invisible
in the clear water dripping into my vein.

A miracle of modern science
my life to Fleming, I do owe
he toiled over dishes touched with bugs
and found what stopped their spread.

And now that battle occurs within me
hidden in my body
drugs that stop the spread of bugs
an army marching through my blood.

The full bag is now shrinking down in size

I watch some bubbles travelling down
pushed by flow, from on high
and feel a glimmer of concern.

What if bubbles coalesce and move into my arm
then whizz around my heart to lung
and back again to heart, then brain
surely, by then, they will dissolve.

But, what if not, and the bubbles join to
block some vital artery supply
the bubbles edge towards my arm
and Jaws film music, worm holes within my ear
as inch by inch, my imminent demise approaches.

Tucked inside the bubble, the shark
fin nears with open jaw
nearer, and nearer, to my hanging arm
rows of teeth now wide apart
alarm bells ring as my finger hits a
blood red button at my side.

A hand appears and bubbles halt,
inches from their entrance
Jaws now closed and turned around
a massive body slides on by
a tail fin waves, brushing all my mind.

"It's OK now," my saviour amity
nurse does whisper calmly
as they tap the tubing upright,

releasing bubble to the air
"Needs a lot of bubbles to blow your brain
and there is a catch all air trap sited in your arm."

"It's only those with holes in heart
that need to worry
and they have a sieve for all those airy bubbles."
My thudding heart slows to a steady pace
and my patients' calm acceptance
resumes with sleep.

December 2022

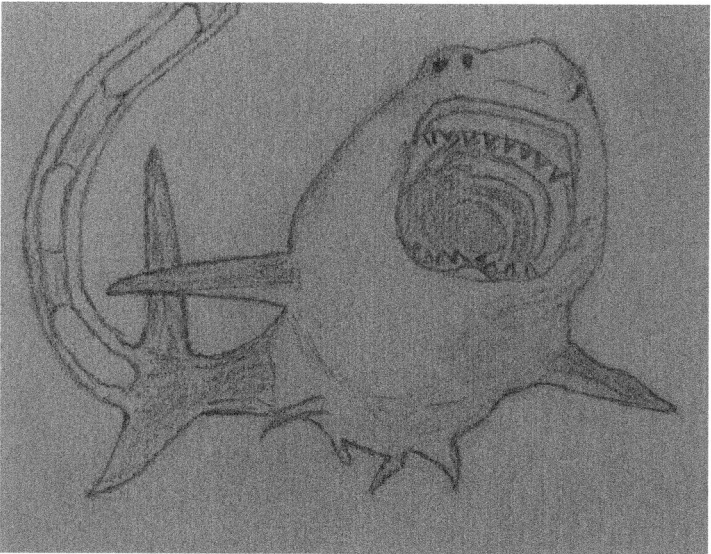

MUSIC ON THE WARDS

Drowsy now in hospital bed, I hear a beeping
a steady soothing beep, at heart-beat rate
in rhythm with the upstroke tracing
on the screen above my head.

A distant call alarm now starts
summoning help to a nearby bed
and beside me the drip stand starts away
with a more urgent tone and pace.

Not to be outdone, the bed pump monitor
warns of deflation with a beep or two
an orchestra of beeps with an air pump rumble
and a background murmur of voices rising.

Accompanied by those familiar
instruments of percussion
closing food tray cymbals, door handle
rattle, sink side gurgle
a slamming door, a cough nearby,
occasionally a wheeze
a cacophony rising to a crescendo.

Now, with a new more strident voice
a forceful warning of impending doom
louder and louder, I jolt up from bed alert
hands fumbling the drip stand for a switch

to silence, or destroy, the raging machine.

Worried now the drip pump is exploding
I push it far across the room and crouch down low
nurses run in, a new unknown noise
and deftly defuse the, now silent, culprit
my alarm clock in from home.

December 2022

*Yes, a true story and my apologies it happened
twice. Second time three nurses ran in to our six-
bay bed area with worried expressions — sorry!
The hospital ward really is noisy and it is such
a relief when the noise drops. There are eye
masks and headphones to borrow or to pass
to those with televisions on full volume.*

NIGHT 2

The day had earlier revealed a large window to my right, with blue sky views. Now covered by a blind, my attention turns to the occupants. The ringleader I have mentally nicknamed Broadcast Bill based on a loud voice and keenness to recount all he has been told. He is in line of sight, hard to ignore, but somehow engaging, drawing me in. Probing to find out my diagnosis, occupation, and age. Evasion with diversion to other topics is the order of the day for myself.

The court room setting of six beds allows close monitoring of the proceeds by everyone. All those present have lost a small or large part of their limbs due to lack of blood supply. Fellow casualties in the war against blood vessel disease. In almost all cases this is due to smoking. Firmly asserted as a cause by the nurses and vehemently denied by the owners of these limbs, it seems a lost cause saying anything. I wisely avoid the topic.

Broadcast Bill has difficulty getting his announcements out at times, due to his smoking induced lung disease, which he is certain has nothing to do with his *ciggies*. In fact, he says he has more phlegm since stopping three days ago. A common observation it seems. He misses that first smoke of the morning, which helps him clear his lung of its protective phlegm.

NIGHT 3

Settling in now and adjusting to the constant barrage of discussion I find myself adding the atmosphere as one of the only mobile patients still holding onto an intact set of limbs. I chat to the artist in the group who is busy using the ward biro to create a mass of curly headed face portraits from memory. The latest football scores are bartered with cricket scores across the bay, each asserting the best teams with self-assured knowledge. Musicians names and song titles flow across the floor in another direction...

"You must listen to..."
"You will really like..."

Then with a wave of the hand it is all change. My observation bed bay is needed for another customer and the lead nurse apologizes for the rapid move. Minutes later I am sitting in the corridor with occasional glimpses of my ejected bed piled with rapidly gathered bags. My replacement seems worse off than me with only a mattress on the floor. I guess he is confused and at risk of falling out of his bed. The observation bay purpose now becomes clearer to me with its good views from all directions.

I now sit on a single footstool in an empty bed space, like a forlorn evacuee at a railway station. By some bizarre twist the consultant ward round appears. My health is discussed amidst the maelstrom of a room change with me on a stool on an empty stage. The entourage moves on and I am left now with a distinct lack of the supper, which my new roommates had been consuming enthusiastically, whilst watching my stage show.

I go in search of a few morsels and a kindly caterer takes pity on me with a slice of toast and marmalade. I start eating this on the corner of an alcove table in the corridor. Not for long, it seems, as space is at a premium and the physiotherapists elbow in. They mutter about speaking in code, but I sense ejection and return to a cluttered bed now discarded at an angle in its allocated space.

My five new roommates seem angelically quiet, happy for brief introductions, at peace with their books, and shorter leg lengths. Calmness pervades with the din of the party room now a distant murmur.

MEDICAL INTERLUDE

Here follows a doctor patient perspective on medications given. Do dip out if it is too much.

Pain control seems to depend on pain killers and not moving. Not moving at all is hard and unhealthy, so it is a balance of the two. Breathing and moving in bed are recommended essentials.

<u>Control of painkillers empowers</u>
Knowing a boost of painkiller can be given by patient directed administration (PDA), with a press of a button, gives confidence, and is such a relief. I had Fentanyl. There was an upper limit to the dose, which could only be given at greater than five-minute intervals.

<u>Withdrawal symptoms</u>
At each medication change there is the risk of pain worsening or withdrawal symptoms, but you might also feel better. Off Fentanyl it was amazing how my head felt clearer. Oxycodone caused less constipation than morphine and dihydrocodeine. Stopping 30mg dihydrocodeine was a shock with headaches and many loose toilet visits for several days.

<u>Always remember the laxatives</u>

Movicol laxative is memorable for an off-putting salty taste, and I wondered if prunes might be just as good. Use everything.

Pressure on the wound

At first it helps to hold an abdominal wound together with a long, rolled towel wrapped around the body and pulled tight.

Later localised pressure with a rolled towel helped more, once the wound had started to heal.

Don't forget heat or cold. Water bottles can be lovely if not too hot. They can also act as a wedge to hold up the tum when lying on one side. Amazingly a room temperature bottle heats with body warmth and becomes cosy.

Safe place

It helps to have a safe place visualised in your mind. A happy place from past memory perhaps. See it, hear it, feel it, taste it, and smell it. See the colours, hear the sounds, feel the warmth, taste the drinks, smell the grass. If you go there just as the anaesthetic hits you might just wake up thinking about it still.

A NIGHT-TIME VISITATION

An angel appears by my hospital bed
a shadow in the low night light
"Sorry," quietly murmured
now, I know it is time to go.

I am ready, things in order
bags sorted and mentally accepting
goodbyes all earlier, have been said
it is hard for nurses to, to say farewell.

And then give a welcome smile
to the next person in my space
but my space is needed, I must now go
and leave this place of refuge.

Suddenly, a posse of nursing cavalry arrives
all keen to move my bed and locker
as I pile my bags upon my mattress high
scanning round for kit and cards that I have missed.

It feels that I am flying on my bed
through swinging doors and long lit up alleyways
a magic carpet trip of surreal experience
landing me in another world.

Nurses wave a welcome here
as my bed starts docking in its bay

a few wakeful patients say hello
whilst mooring wires secure my vessel to the wall.

The beep and hiss of reconnected bed resumes
and nurses relocate my kit around
this ward seems quieter here, I note
as I settle into gently rocking, air puffed, bed.

December 2022

There is a constant awareness that you might need to be moved at any time. It was easier just to be constantly ready with bags packed. When the nurse asks, everything is thrown on, and you go off on the bed. In England a person's home is said to be their castle. In hospital it is the bed that is the castle and your home.

NIGHT 4

Either side of me there are now empty beds, their occupants having recovered sufficiently to head home. My own condition causes sufficient concern to keep me in, but not confined to, my bed. It seems this might be a quiet night until two admissions arrive close on the wheels of each other.

A loud voice announces, to my left, he has no clothes to go home in. They are lost. A louder disembodied voice booms, from my right, through similar, closed, blue curtains that he has lost all his belongings as well.

Both demand rapid action, each competing in volume, with me caught in the verbal crossfire in the middle. The nurse moves from one bay to the other trying to complete observations and answer questions about what is to be done "immediately, now, this minute".

To the left, demands to call the police emerge and are taken up enthusiastically to my right. Right goes quieter as his demands have been trumped by Left with the addition of a comprehensive range of expletives, many beginning with F.

I catch a glimpse of large buttocks framed in operative gown as Left stumps across the floor, trailing blood from his neatly dressed foot. Nurse advice that this is not the best post operation management is lost amidst the tirade of verbal abuse. A request to put in an intravenous cannula to give antibiotics is met by flat refusal, as the nurse backs away startled.

Eventually, both regain their clothes and belongings, but insist on making complaints. An efficient, calm, official looking person arrives with paper, clipboard, and pen. Later, when asked about their seniority, a nurse confirms that they are the ward housekeeper.

As a patient I am much more aware of the disturbances at night and sometimes the day. Three burly security team members have to attend the ward round one morning as a portly, younger, man very aggressively complains to the consultant that he waited almost four hours in a bed to be seen the previous night.

One evening I am confused by my painkillers and misinterpret the ward conversations. I ask a nurse what is happening as it sounds like a couple of patients have died in the fighting.

"Do you know where you are?" they ask.

I reply, "High Dependency."

And they respond, "Well, there you are."

They go on to explain that no one has died. One person wants to be alone in a room, whilst the others are confused and want to leave.

When I later visit High Dependency, I discover it is much smaller than my hazy mind recalls. Behind my bed has, in reality, been a solid wall, where I swear many other beds have existed with nurses walking back and forth to them.

THE WARD TEAM

We come to you, shaky and uncertain
facing, perhaps, our final curtain
you explain away our worries and fears
soothing our path as operation time nears.

The ward is neat, and clean, and organized
moments of chaos are brief,
expected and scrutinized
a calmness and routine does pervade
pushing aside the awaited fall of blade.

But the listening and explaining is
what makes a ward so great
a moment longer taken, prepared to hear, and wait
a smile, a joke, a word of comfort sought
staving off concerns about the battle fought.

You do this many times each day
so often, indeed, that many would not even say
how important a simple explanation can be
to us, a grain of gold, amidst a sand filled sea.

Remember then, when we have flown
the patients change, and not all
problems are solved or known
but 'tis your humanity and kindness that will show
the way forward that we, all, must

learn, retain and go.

December 2022

Fear and uncertainty are inevitable as a patient, yet they are handled by calm ward staff as a matter of day-to-day existence. Staff have a relaxed façade of masked brilliance, but for some the stress can show. Sometimes through a protective remoteness. Others by escape of tremor or voice change. Support is then needed, as today's NHS is also a hothouse of stress, overwork and underpay.

ABLATION TREATMENT—
18 YEARS EARLIER

Calm and inevitable at each stage. Decision and preparations made already, so there was nothing to do but wait for the next step. Step by step, closer to the start. Intravenous access inserted, bloods taken, and gown change. Never sure how to do these gowns up at the back. Why doesn't someone say. Perhaps no one knows. Offered and grateful for paper knickers.

Transported on bed down the corridor. Regal wave at the ready. Victim to the altar cheered on by varying emotions of others. Pity, sympathy and, for some, on longer waits, envy. My wife beside me to the final doorway then it is goodbye. Brief and lost amidst the moment. No need for carefully prepared words. All said and unsaid in the preceding hours.

I chat to the nurse as I wait. Then it is my turn. My bed wheeled through. I go in backwards unable to see the room ahead. The chamber of my torture I think to myself. The hidden depths shielded in lead. I meekly shuffle across the board on to the operating table. Ten or more screens face me. A console greets me like last week's Live Aid concert with Bob Geldof, a woofer box with plugs and sockets all over.

I wonder why I am lying here so quietly. To those around deep in concentration I have become an object to plug it, stick on and wire up. Cold plates seem to be attached all over me. Double neck pillow, lower back roll and behind knee supports provided as requested. The iodine slapped on and drapes laid over me. Head turned to the left so I can't see any faces. The drape is now nearly over my face, unexpected oxygen mask applied, but still calm, detached, clinically interested. A sting of anesthetic in the groin and then the only sensation is of an occasional push with slight ache in the loin. The screen in front of me now shows three wires waving around in my blood stream. Three wires inside me curling around my heart. Mentally I encourage the doctor in her efforts to unfurl the lead. Draw back and advance she does with success. I thank her in silent relief. The catheter lead tips are beating within the heart - my heart. Diazepam offered and accepted. A little float, but no difference otherwise.

A pause whilst the great surgeon is awaited. I understand why, but ask out of politeness. Their voice is reassuring and the final step is slotted into place. The catheters cross the inner wall of my heart without me noticing. My heart triggers off in its usual pattern of irregular beats to the satisfaction of the surgeon. Ah, found the trigger! Then the Midazolam kicks in with morphine. Morphine strangely makes my limbs ache without any high or buzz. Occasional pains shoot to my lower teeth then build up in my chest until I feel I must say something. Three or four times I think this happens. Dose chart suggests so. One, two, three then four hours pass by. Ten thousand pounds of time and resource they said.

Then I recall sheets and plastic pads being pulled back. Then strangely nothing. No exit, no return to the ward. Then my lovely wife beside my bed encouraging me to lie still on my back. Backache becoming the focus. Then eventually I can turn on my side. Relief and sleep, I think.

September 2005

Every moment throughout a hospital people experience lifesaving and life-changing experiences. All around you day and night.

A FORTUNATE VACCINE VEX -
COVID PANDEMIC 2021

It's Pfizer versus Oxford Astra Zeneca just now
some think they have a choice somehow
others have to take first come,
first served, the decision is no sum.

It seems the choice, if given, is not so clear
mRNA from 1990s study is now here
but viral injected DNA has been around for years
decision making, and false news,
just stoke up all the fears.

The short-term side effects are
similar, the studies say
and the long-term, for both, is unknown, anyway
Pfizer more faff as frozen stored, a
rush to give, once melted out
whilst Zeneca in fridge it sits, with
time to book and think about.

And Pfizer's more expensive too,
with Zeneca low cost
Pfizer needs to be mixed, a sixth dose can be lost
whilst Zeneca is ready made, eight doses to a vial
moving it to house and home, is much less of a trial.

But remember how fortunate we all are

as vaccines cure and hold the exit door ajar
a miracle of science to smallpox Jenner we owe
a glimpse of light above, in tunnel dark below.

The solution, I suggest, for you and me
is much easier, as you will see
P is at middle and A or Z at ends of English alphabet
so just go with what you're given,
and accept it's what you get.

June 2021

You may recall the debate about which vaccine
was best, when nobody really knew, and we
just had to be grateful for a solution.

WHY ME?

Why me?
That it should be
suspected infection
of unknown conception.

No bug discovered
yet every test covered
sore gum a month ago
a cause or not, we'll never know.

A fall during the day
night pain, did not go away
persistent right lower back
sitting, moving or flat in the sack.

So GP colleague I see
and blood test, abnormal for me
ultrasound it is
and to hospital I whizz.

CT scan to do the same day
a crisis in the main blood vessel highway
the lower aorta is worn
wider, inflamed and partially torn.

A life changing shock
that my fitness does mock

four weeks later I head home
only to be called back, urgently, by phone.

It's widening now
needs replacement somehow
that blood pumping highway
has developed a byway.

A replacement is major and bold
using a covering of ox heart, I'm told
in operating theatre, I now lie
prepared in mind for all and goodbye.

January 2023

UNEXPECTED BUSES

If I should be hit by a bus, think of me,
and remember the good times – Waterloo
sunsets, Hamble river walks, blackberry
picking, archery, badminton, sailing, mirror
dinghy, Jersey, seaside days, campervans,
sunshine, garden games, birthday parties,
weddings, summer parties and hugs.

There is never a good way to wave goodbye, and
a bit of me just wants to hand write to every one
of you in my life. A special letter of advice, hugs
and love to carry you onward through it all.

You are amazing, a miracle and so remember how
incredible you are and how much you are loved.
I have always loved you, love you now, and love you
ever more. And that is not just my lovely Louise,
but all of you since you popped into our existence.

I am sure I will be with you in our shared
memories and continue as part of you, as part
of your very genetic core. Our relationship will
change, but I will always be there with you.
Love you always, whatever.

THE AWAKENING

Ok! I am here still
is this heaven or earthly home?
I can feel
arms here, legs there.

Breathing ok, no pain there
throat, not sore
nose clear, no tube there
not too bad, I survived.

Later...
discoveries
as yet, unseen
another tube or two.

Tube removal
slowly, day by day
each a step to recovery
twelve or more tubes I count.

"Deep breathe, hold, exhale," they say.
"Gosh, that was a long one"
Arm over arm, winching out
"I enjoyed that," says my satisfied nurse.

First mirror
shaky shower

cautious movements
a few telltale holes remain.

Dare I glimpse or touch the scar
brief look, then longer gaze
a new zip lane friend for life
cause a myth, or story to be told.

January 2023

MONKEY ARMS

I shower with one arm up high,
pressed against the wall
some of you may wonder why and
others just do not care
it stops me toppling when eyes are closed, I grant
especially, when ballerina posed
upon one soapy limb.

But no, as those in health may guess, it
is to protect my special PICC*
a tube that runs from arm to heart, inside
and delivers special medications,
with uninterrupted ease
a lifeline, whose exit must avoid
the wet or risky bugs.

So I stand, like woolly monkey,
right hand held up high
my left hand curled right under,
patting soap into its armpit
admitting grunting noises, as I
stretch my body round
and try to reach all areas, with that
right side pointing skyward.

Tried all I have, from plastic bags or cling film to
clever shop-bought tubes, with unforgiving

rubber seals, gaping at each end
but all to no avail, as holding up that
arm, out of shower's spray
was still the best and simplest,
chimp-like trick I know.

So monkey pose it is, that I recommend to all
a nonchalant lean, on the top, of the showering wall
ignominious, but effective, when
indoors, if you please
but not if your shower is open,
and sits in jungle trees.

*PICC Peripheral Intravenous Central Catheter

Jan 2023

*The first shower after an operation is always an event
and usually a success to celebrate. Intravenous lines
and other tubes add a certain challenge in addition
to some dizziness, poor balance and weaker muscles.
As the alarm cord sign says, "Please call, don't fall."*

UNWELL TO STILL SORE ON MOVING

Slowly roll on bed, push upright
wait and check
head muzzy and dizzy.

Arms and legs ok today
chair the objective
seems far away
relief once seated.

Tired and sleepy
slowed up with pains
just able to read
will it always be like this?

Four weeks on:

Hey what! No pain just now
just the usual aches of age reappearing
alert and with it, I feel
less tired, less sleepy by day.

Suddenly, I've turned a corner
has been a few days now
on the mend, hope is there
life is good, future beckons once again.

February 2023

THE LONG C WORD

Oh mercy me
Did I not see
The laxatives I need
No
No No
No No No
No No No No No   No No No
No No No No No No No No No No   No No No
No No No No No No No No No No No No No No
No   No
No No No No No No No No No No No No No No No
No No
No No No No No No No No Yes No No No No No
No No No No
No No No No No No No No No No No No No No No
No No
No No No No No No No No No No No No No No No
No No No No No No No No No No No No No No No
No No No No No No No No No   No No No
No No No No No   No No No
No Yes No
Yes Yes
Yes

A GOOD NIGHT'S KIP

A good night's sleep is what I need
if not, a negative experience becomes a seed
for thoughts and worries about all life
dreams become real, persist and are full of strife.

Then, drugs reduce, antibiotics stop, painkillers too
so withdrawl now, with headache,
and lots to pee and poo
a week or more to settle these
until a normal me, in hope, I seize.

Awake all day, by strange, good fortune
and late to bed, still fear of wakeful night-time tune
but there is relief as a merciful
Prometheus of sleep emerges
no nightmares, or hours awake, so
hope within me surges.

February 2023

SLUGGISH MIND

Clarity of thought eludes me just now
I struggle to get from musing to how
I know it's the illness, but frustration exists
time's passing me by, as this
vacuous lethargy persists.
My mind muddles on, reliving events
of internal changes, tubes, injections and stents
tensions of body and mind cluster
in woesome disorder
I'm digesting the past, in an attempt to reorder.
Glimmers of hope arise at odd times
insights pop up to record, on paper lines
late evening seems best, with glimpses of clarity
longer, as daylight moves onto a
springtime of parity.
And now, joy arises, on my first full day
of awakeness throughout, pushing confusion away
as tasks, texts and emails shrink under my gaze
the effort to do no longer the trigger to laze.
I've aged I know
but the change today, makes me glow
with a movement of youth and brightness in mind
the contrast, makes me shout, that life can be kind.

February 2023

HELLO SCAR

Hello, my scar, that's new to me
sitting there for all to see
a neon purple strip light
reminder of that recent fight.

Initially raw red, scabbed, it seemed
a puckered mountain range, I dreamed
with time it flattened, smoothing away my fear
a livid road map of my route to here.

As gingerly I touch
wary, least I press too much
sensation varies from nausea to sting
fading memory of the pains it could bring.

A friend for life
focus for loving caress, by caring wife.

February 2023

MY ROAD MAP SCAR

My scar runs straight down
from Midlands to the south
with a westward detour
on the ring road around
belly button down.

Then an eastward slant
before the hillcrest turn
towards the west again
and a steady downhill
to the coast.

March 2023

HOME FROM WORK

The NHS worker is back at home
parents here, so not alone
a busy, hectic day, since morning hospital, she went
and now her bubbly energy is briefly spent.

Slow moving and heavy eyed
she sinks into the chair, beside
parents, their listening position assume
as reheated supper, their offspring, does consume.

As food her, stomach fills
with calories, energy gradually instils
slowly tales of daytime events unfold
family listen and empathise, as told.

Of stories, staffing changes and close shaves
as multi patient care she paves
of people's anger, sadness, dismay and tears
how her words and smiles helped
soothe away their fears.

All anonymised, no names or details tell
in confidence she looks after patient info well
a counsellor gets monthly supervisory support
yet doctor, pharmacy or nurse, only
given if disaster court.

So let's all help our healthcare workers in their role
give them both time for work, and
to refresh their soul
remind them of the good they have done
and the day's successes, fought and won.

March 2023

ABOUT THE PATIENT

Prof. Mark Rickenbach

A GP working at Park and St Francis surgery near Southampton for thirty years, who started out as a nursing auxiliary. He holds GP and hospital consultant qualifications with a PhD in healthcare education quality and a keen interest in continuity of care. Mark provided medical care in Australia, Hong Kong, Swaziland and London — where he was also a 2012 Olympic games maker. He has an interest in research and teaching, linked to University of Winchester, with sixty related publications. With deeply heartfelt thanks to Louise, who was always there throughout illness and operation. Supported by their children Adam, Amelia and Lydia.

docrick.co.uk
mark.rickenbach@nhs.net

Vascular surgery wards cover a whole range of illness and different patient personalities, because so many diseases can affect the blood vessels. Diabetes, heart disease, dementia and social deprivation are all frequent visitors. So the team has to be able to cope with social issues, confusion, and complex leg ulcers in addition to caring for pre- and post-operative patients. Everyone contributes to the running of the ward. Day-to-day it is often those working nine to five, delivering meals or the house keeping who provide social continuity for each patient.

Health Care Assistants may find time to encourage patients whilst doing observations. Nurses keep a watchful eye for changes between medication rounds. Pharmacists monitor those medications. Physiotherapists and Occupational therapists help with rehabilitation to get home. Chaplains provide spiritual support and counselling. Consultant teams visit daily to plan overall direction, undertake procedures and expert surgery. Then, once discharged there is the hospital at home team, GPs and all the primary care team. A whole bunch of people with a wide range of experience and expertise interacting together to support their patients. But who looks after them?

With thanks again to all those who looked after me from November 2022 to March 2023. You are all amazing, caring and work so hard under the daily pressure of the NHS.

Thank you so much.

TIM SAUNDERS PUBLICATIONS
poetry, fiction and memoir

"Everybody has a book in them," according to
journalist Christopher Hitchens (1949 to 2011)

Do you have a book you would like to publish?

Email. tsaunderspubs@gmail.com

For more information visit:
tsaunderspubs.weebly.com

Regular writing opportunities including monthly
challenges and the Paul Cave Prize for Literature

Printed in Great Britain
by Amazon